The Creature Vanishes

By Charles Higgins and
Regina Higgins
Illustrated by Thea Kliros

Modern Curriculum Press
Parsippany, New Jersey

1-800-321-3106
www.pearsonlearning.com

Contents

For Frances and Charles

Chapter 1

What Was That?

The day of the big field trip had finally arrived. It was a cool spring day with blue skies and bright sunshine. The school Ecology Club planned to spend the day exploring the forests and streams of nearby Big Mountain Park.

The school van stopped in the main parking lot. Luke Williams hurried to help unload the club's equipment when suddenly he heard a rustling sound in the bushes. He quickly looked up and caught sight of a tiny reddish-brown animal.

"Look, a chipmunk!" he yelled, as the small furry animal scooted away.

"We'll see a lot of those little fellows," said Mrs. Delgado. "The park is a good place for them to live." Mrs. Delgado was a teacher and also the advisor for the Ecology Club, sometimes called EcoKids for short.

"That's why we're here, Mrs. D!" said Steve Alvarez. Steve and Luke had asked Mrs. Delgado if they could bring the school's video camera. They were hoping to film some animals and their habitats, or living places.

Another project the club planned to do was to test the water in the Flint River. In Big Mountain Park the river was just a stream, much smaller than the river it became as it flowed through River City.

Mr. Baxter, the park naturalist and ranger, helped Karen Harper and Wendy Asato set up the testing equipment. "We'll use pH paper to check the pH level of the water," Mr. Baxter explained. "The pH measures certain chemicals in the water. It can tell us whether or not the water is healthy for plants and animals."

As Mr. Baxter watched, Wendy dipped a small, clear glass bottle into the river and filled it with water. "Now dip the pH paper," he said, handing her a small pink strip. "It will change color."

Wendy took the strip of special paper and dipped
it carefully in the water. When she took it out
again, she looked to see what color it was.

"Let's match it to the colors on the pH color chart," said Mr. Baxter. "We're looking for a high pH, somewhere around seven. That's normal water. A low pH is acidic, meaning the water has a lot of acid in it. That is not so healthy. Acidic water can kill plants and harm or kill the animals that live in the water, such as fish and frogs."

"What would make the water acidic?" Karen wanted to know.

"Good question," Mr. Baxter told her. "Different things can change the pH. Pollution from someone dumping waste into the river could lower the pH. If there's smoke or other pollution in the air when it rains, the rain can carry those chemicals into the river water. It could even be something natural, such as an underground volcano, but that would be very unusual around here."

"Look!" Wendy called out. "It's right near the seven! That means the water is good for animals and plants."

6.0 6.2 6.4 66 68 7.0 7.2 7.4 7.6

pH TEST COLOR CHART

Karen opened her Nature Log notebook. She wrote down the date and place of the experiment and noted the result. She was always careful to record everything.

"That's a good piece of news to put on the club's Web site, Karen," Mrs. Delgado said.

Mr. Baxter turned around. "The EcoKids have a Web site?" he asked

Karen nodded. "Mrs. Delgado is helping us. We're calling it The River City Almanac. We're going to post all kinds of news about River City."

"Well, that's great!" Mr. Baxter said. "You can tell everyone that the pH level in our river is safe for the animals that live here."

"Mrs. Delgado!" shouted Luke. "May we use the video camera now? We found a squirrel on a tree over here!"

Mrs. Delgado laughed as she got the video camera from the school bus. "Sure you may, Luke, but don't shout, or you'll scare it away!"

"Sorry," Luke mumbled. He was just so excited that he was in a hurry to do everything.

Luke tried to remember what Mrs. Delgado had taught him about using the video camera. He raised the camera to his face and found the squirrel through the viewfinder.

The squirrel darted over to a tall tree, clinging to the bark with its claws. Luke followed its movements with the video camera. Steve was going to narrate the video, so he stood nearby and talked about the animal and its habitat.

"Squirrels live in Big Mountain Park," Steve began to speak slowly and clearly. "The trees and bushes give them shelter, and the river is nearby for water. Squirrels are plant eaters that especially like nuts. Since this squirrel is climbing a tree, I guess it's going to try to find some food."

Feeling like a real filmmaker, Luke followed the squirrel with the camera as it scurried up the trunk. When the squirrel disappeared into the high branches, Luke zoomed in to get a close-up. Then he backed up to get a better view. Maybe he could get a shot of the squirrel sitting on a branch in the tree. Suddenly he saw something big moving quickly through the bushes just past the tree.

"Steve!" Luke gasped.

"I'm right here," said Steve. He was standing next to Luke.

"What's that?" asked Luke. He kept his eye on the viewfinder and pointed the camera toward the clump of bushes where he'd seen the movement.

For a split second, Luke and Steve both had a clear sighting of a tall, furry figure. Then it was gone. What had they seen?

Chapter 2

Signs of Bigfoot

"Wow!" shouted Steve, losing his usual calm. "Did you see that? I've never seen anything like that before! It must be some kind of gorilla!"

"It's right here in Big Mountain Park!" added Luke excitedly.

"What's going on?" asked Mrs. Delgado. She had heard Luke and Steve talking.

Steve and Luke both spoke at once. "We saw a big, tall gorilla! A huge, big, hairy . . ."

"Whoa, calm down!" said Mrs. Delgado.

Mr. Baxter, Wendy, and Karen came over to find out what the excitement was all about.

"I was videotaping the squirrel," Luke began, "and I saw something moving way over there." He pointed to the bushes.

"I saw it, too," Steve added. "It looked like a big, tall gorilla."

"Gorillas usually walk on all fours," Wendy pointed out. "Did it walk on four legs or two?"

"It was walking like a person," Luke said, "but it was a lot bigger than a person."

15

"It was furry, too," Steve said, "like a furry animal."

Mrs. Delgado listened with interest. "Well, it sounds as if it might have been a bear." She turned to the naturalist. "What do you think, Mr. Baxter?"

Mr. Baxter thought for a minute. "It could have been a bear. Bears sometimes rise up on two legs. Yet they're rarely seen around here."

"It wasn't a bear!" Luke shook his head stubbornly. "I know what a bear looks like!"

"You said it was far off, Luke. Sometimes your eyes can play tricks on you," Mrs. Delgado said.

"I did see it for only a second or two," Luke admitted. He was disappointed to think his great sighting was just a trick of his eyes.

Mr. Baxter smiled. "You're not the first person to see something strange around here. Some people say they've seen Bigfoot in these woods."

"Bigfoot?" asked Karen. "I thought that was just a story people made up."

"It's a legend that goes back many years," Mr. Baxter told her. "The creature we call Bigfoot or Sasquatch even appears in Native American legends that go back hundreds of years. No one has ever caught a Sasquatch, but some people claim they've found evidence that the creature really exists around here."

17

"What do you mean, evidence?" Steve asked.

"Physical evidence would be some kind of clue or proof, such as a footprint or other sign," Mr. Baxter told them. "I don't have to see a squirrel to know when one's been in my yard. I might see footprints, chewed acorn shells, or holes in the ground where nuts or bulbs have been dug up, or even a bit of gray fluff from a squirrel's tail stuck on a thorn bush. That's evidence of the squirrel."

"Let's look for Bigfoot evidence!" shouted Luke. He hurried up the hill toward the bushes where he had seen the creature. The others followed him.

"We'll find proof. I just know it," Wendy reassured Luke.

Luke, Steve, Wendy, and Karen walked slowly and carefully, looking for signs of the strange creature. Suddenly Luke pointed to a spot up ahead where the bushes had been flattened.

"Look!" he cried. "Bigfoot must have moved through here really fast!"

The kids gathered around. Mrs. Delgado and Mr. Baxter looked at the bushes closely.

"It does appear that way," Mr. Baxter said. "It could have been a bear. Bears crash through bushes that way all the time."

Steve groaned. "Bigfoot must have left a better clue! Can't we find something else?"

"Were you still videotaping when you saw the creature?" Mrs. Delgado asked. "Whatever you saw might be on the videotape."

Luke sighed. "I already tried replaying the tape through the viewfinder, but the image is too small." He pointed to the videocamera slung over his shoulder. "Maybe when we play it on the television in the school media center, we'll see something."

"I wish I could have seen it," Karen said.

"I wish it had stayed longer!" Wendy added.

"Maybe it lives somewhere up there on the mountain," Steve said. "Maybe it saw us, got scared, and ran home."

"Bigfoot's a slippery creature," Mr. Baxter agreed. "It can come and go without a trace."

Suddenly Luke looked up. "Maybe not," he whispered. He stepped aside and pointed to the ground. The sun hadn't been able to reach the shady spot beneath the bushes, and it was still damp from a recent rain. There, in the soft mud, was a clear trail of enormous footprints.

"Maybe that video *will* have something to show you," Mr. Baxter said.

Chapter 3

The Media Center

It was late when they got back. The next day Luke could hardly wait until school was over and he could head for the Media Center. He was finally going to be able to see the videotape he'd shot on the big screen.

Susan, his older sister, was already there, working on the computer. She spent afternoons at the Media Center working with Mrs. Delgado and helping the kids set up their River City Almanac Web site.

Luke told Susan that he also wanted to add a note to the site. It would ask if anyone knew anything about the strange creature he and Steve had seen.

"Other people may have seen something that could help us track down the creature," Luke said.

Susan first helped Luke to set up a response key on the site. It asked people to post their own news on the site. Then Susan's fingers flew across the computer keyboard. "Wanted," she typed, "information about any unusual sightings in Big Mountain Park."

"There," Susan told Luke. "If people have anything to tell us, all they have to do is click on this and type in their comments. Then they will be automatically posted on the Web site."

"That looks great!" Karen said, coming in with Wendy and Steve. They were there to get the school VCR ready to show the videotape Luke had shot. After a few minutes, Steve said, "OK, Luke, it's ready to roll."

"Now let's see if we can get a good look at Bigfoot, Luke," Mrs. Delgado told him.

Luke pressed the play button. Everyone watched as he fast-forwarded the tape to the part where the squirrel ran up the tree.

"Now," Luke pointed to the screen. "I saw it moving over there."

"I see something!" Wendy said excitedly.

"Something," Mrs. Delgado agreed, "but what?"

Luke hit the rewind button and started the tape again. "Watch for it over there, near the bushes," he told his friends.

Once again they saw a blurry figure walking upright. It moved very fast, and the picture jumped up and down, so it was hard to see clearly. Almost as soon as they spotted the creature, it seemed to disappear into the woods.

"If only I'd held the camera steady," Luke said unhappily. He hung his head and sighed.

"It is too bad, Luke," Mrs. Delgado said, "but don't blame yourself. You were taken by surprise, and Bigfoot didn't stay around long enough for a good picture."

"Bigfoot's just a slippery creature, like Mr. Baxter said," added Steve.

"You can see *something* moving," Karen said. "If it isn't Bigfoot, what could it be?"

"Let me see it," said a voice. It was Luke and Susan's mother, who had just arrived to pick up the kids from school.

Susan wheeled over and restarted the tape.

"It's blurry because the camera was shaking," Luke told his mother, "but look! Remember the creature I told you about last night? See it walking into the woods?"

Dr. Williams watched carefully, then rewound the tape and played it back again.

"I think I know what you're seeing," she said finally.

"What is it?" the kids all cried at once.

Dr. Williams folded her arms. "Well, one of the things we've been working on at my lab is a special suit for extreme weather conditions."

"Extreme weather?" Wendy asked. "What do you mean? Is that like extreme sports?" Wendy was a big fan of extreme sports. Her dream was to someday snowboard down a nearby mountain that could only be reached by helicopter.

Dr. Williams laughed. She said, "The suit we're designing is for extreme *science*. It will make it possible for scientists to work longer in harsh conditions, such as the extreme cold in Antarctica."

"What does that have to do with Bigfoot?" Steve wanted to know.

"Well, the suit is made of a dark woolly material, and it can make a person look very tall because of the padded boots that go with it. I also know that some of my lab assistants have been testing the suit to see how well it allows movement," Dr. Williams explained.

"Mom, are you trying to tell us it was one of your lab assistants Luke saw?" Susan asked.

"Well, we did talk about testing the suit in Big Mountain Park to see how well it worked for a person climbing up or down steep rocky hills for long periods of time," Dr. Williams said.

"Bigfoot was furry," Steve pointed out. "Is the suit furry?"

Dr. Williams thought for a minute. "Not really, but it might look that way from far off."

"I know what I saw!" cried Luke.

"Me, too!" added Steve.

Suddenly there was a small beep from the computer. Everyone turned. Susan and Karen went to the computer.

"We've got our first posting from someone!" Karen said. "It's about Bigfoot!"

Chapter 4

Bigfoot's Foot

All the kids gathered around the computer to see the posting on Bigfoot. Susan pointed to the screen and read the message.

Hi! I'm one of the many River City folks who has seen Bigfoot in the park. It was five years ago, just around this time of year. I've been looking for him ever since. Has anyone seen him lately?

"Wow!" cried Steve. "He's seen Bigfoot, just like we have!"

"Who is the message from?" asked Mrs. Delgado.

Susan moved the screen down. "It's from Dr. Carl Vincent."

"Carl Vincent?" Dr. Williams said. "I know him! He works with our lab. He also teaches a course at the college on cryptozoology."

"I know what zoology is," Wendy said. "That's the study of animals. I've never heard of *cryptozoology*, though."

"Well, *crypto* means 'hidden or mysterious,'" Susan told her.

"I knew that," Steve added. "The codes my grandfather and I use to send secret messages to each other are also called cryptography. Papa Tito told me that means 'hidden writing.'"

"That's right," Dr. Williams said. "Cryptozoology is the study of animals that we can't always see. Sometimes cryptozoologists try to discover whether or not an animal really exists. Many people say they've seen a strange creature in Loch Ness. That's a lake in Scotland. Cryptozoologists have even explored the lake, looking for it."

"That's just like Bigfoot!" Steve said. "A lot of people don't believe Bigfoot really exists, even though lots of people say they've seen him."

"Dr. Vincent says he's seen Bigfoot," Luke said excitedly, "and he studies creatures like Bigfoot. I want to meet Dr. Vincent!"

"Me, too!" added Steve.

"OK, OK," Dr. Williams said, laughing. "I'll call him right now." She moved to a corner of the room, took out her portable telephone, and punched in a number.

Karen had been thinking. "Mrs. Delgado," she asked, "how can a cryptozoologist study an animal if no one has really seen it?"

"All living things leave traces. Remember what Mr. Baxter said, that he didn't have to see a squirrel to know one had been in his yard?" Mrs. Delgado asked. "A footprint, a fossilized egg, or a bit of hair can give a scientist a lot of clues about an animal, even if it died millions of years ago."

"You mean people who study dinosaurs are cryptozoologists?" Steve wanted to know.

"Some of them are," Mrs. Delgado said.

Dr. Williams had finished her phone call. She added, "Dr. Vincent can tell you all about cryptozoology on Saturday."

"We're meeting him Saturday?" Luke yelled. "That's great! Thanks, Mom!"

"Mrs. Delgado said you can learn a lot from a footprint," Steve reminded Luke. "What about Bigfoot's footprints?"

"You might start by making a plaster cast of one of the footprints," Mrs. Delgado suggested. "That would give you a model that shows the size and shape of the foot. In fact, we might go back to the park now, before it gets dark. I'll get what we need." She left for the science room.

"Wait until we show Dr. Vincent a plaster cast of Bigfoot's footprints!" Luke cried.

Mrs. Delgado came back carrying a big box. "Who's ready to go?" she said.

"I AM!" everyone shouted back.

They parked near the spot where the Ecology Club had been on their last visit to the park. Luke led the way to the place where he and Steve had seen Bigfoot. "Here's the tree," he said, pointing.

"The footprints should be over there, under that bush," Steve added, pointing to where Luke was.

"Over here!" Luke called. "See, Mom?"

Dr. Williams bent down to look at the huge footprints. "Hmmm," she murmured, "this does look more like a footprint than a bootprint."

Steve carefully brushed leaves and twigs away from the tracks while Wendy mixed the plaster with water that Mrs. Delgado had brought. Then Karen chose a cardboard ring that fit around one of the footprints and placed it gently in the dirt.

Luke crouched low and poured the plaster into the footprint. He was careful to fill the track and the surrounding earth to the top of the ring.

"It will take a few minutes to harden," Mrs. Delgado told them. "Then we'll be able to bring Bigfoot's footprint home!"

"Did you find other clues?" asked Dr. Williams.

Luke rose to his feet. "Over there," he said, pointing. "See where the bushes have been flattened? That proves that something big came through here in a hurry."

Steve walked over to show Dr. Williams the crushed bushes. Suddenly, he stopped. "Look at this!" he cried. He pointed to something on a bush.

Luke and Susan rushed over. "It's some of Bigfoot's hair!" Luke cried. He reached out to grab it, but Susan stopped him.

"Luke, not only is it very unscientific for you to touch that hair, it could also be dangerous! There might be germs on it that could make you sick," Mrs. Delgado said. Susan nodded.

Luke looked surprised, but his mother agreed with Mrs. Delgado and Susan. "A real scientist would be very careful to avoid contaminating any kind of sample by handling it. That's why we use these," she explained, taking a pair of tweezers and a small plastic bag from her pocket. She used the tweezers to remove the hair from the bush, then carefully bagged the sample.

"We're learning to be real cryptozoologists now," Steve pointed out.

"I think the plaster is ready!" Wendy called.

As everyone watched, Luke carefully lifted the hardened plaster ring from the dirt. It was so large and heavy he had to use both hands to hold it. When he held it up, everyone could see a perfect copy of the huge foot that had made the print on the ground!

"It's sure got the right name!" Karen said, laughing.

"Bigfoot," Luke said, looking at the plaster cast, "where are you?"

Chapter 5

"I Saw Bigfoot!"

The next afternoon, Luke and his friends headed over to the school computer room. Susan was already there, checking the Web site. There were more postings about Bigfoot!

"Look at this!" she called out to them.

I saw Bigfoot last year, one message read. *He was picking berries in the woods in Big Mountain Park. When he saw me, he ran off into the woods.*

"That's what he did when he saw us," Steve said. "He must be shy."

"Let's read another message," said Wendy.

I think people don't understand Bigfoot. I saw him when I was a boy, about 20 years ago. He seemed like a gentle fellow, really. I think he just wants to be left alone.

"Some of the messages say Bigfoot's been living here a long time," Karen said. "Look at what this one says!"

My grandmother lived near Big Mountain over 80 years ago. When she was a girl, she lost her doll in the woods. Early one morning she looked out her window and saw a big, hairy creature carrying her doll toward the house! He put it on the porch and left. It was Bigfoot!

"Wow," said Steve, "I guess Bigfoot's been around a long time."

"He's part of River City history," Karen replied, "or at least stories of Bigfoot are."

"Bigfoot isn't just a story. Look at this," Luke said. The kids moved to the table where Luke had spread a large sheet of paper.

"I found photos of different kinds of tracks in nature books. I traced them onto this paper," he said, pointing.

"Here's a human footprint," Luke said.
"That's big," Karen said.
"Here's a bear footprint," Luke went on.
"Bigger!" Wendy said with a big grin.

"Now here's Bigfoot's footprint." Luke pointed to the last print.

"Wow!" cried Steve. "That's the biggest!"

"Bigfoot's tracks are certainly the biggest of all," Mrs. Delgado agreed.

"Susan! Can we post a picture of these footprints on our Web site?" Karen asked.

"What about posting the video, too?" Luke added. "Maybe someone will see something we don't. It's worth a try."

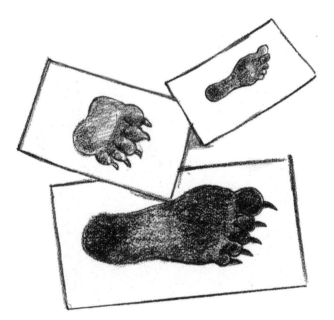

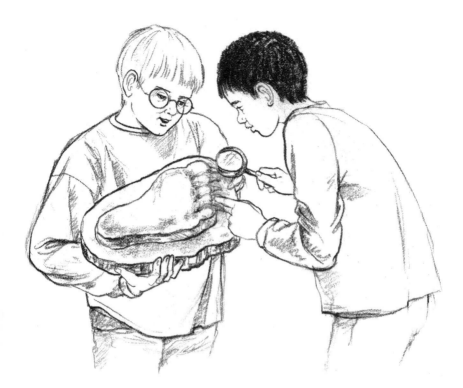

"I can help you do that," Susan told them. She wheeled closer to the computer and began tapping out commands on the keyboard.

Luke looked closely at the cast of Bigfoot's footprint. "Look here, Steve," he said. "It's got five toes, like us, but there are claws on them."

Steve nodded. "Did you find out anything about the hair?"

"No, not yet," Luke replied. "My mom tested the hair at her lab and gave me back the part they didn't use." He pulled the plastic bag out of his backpack. "No one can say for sure what kind of animal it comes from."

"Does your mom still think we saw someone in that suit her lab is making?" asked Steve.

Luke shook his head. "She hasn't been able to talk to any of the people who have been testing the suit, but she still doesn't believe it was Bigfoot."

"Luke!" called Mrs. Delgado. "Someone is really paying attention to our Web site. There's already a message for you!"

"Wow," Luke said. "That was fast." He hurried over to the computer and sat down.

Luke,

Greetings, fellow cryptozoologist!

I've seen your video and the tracks you drew. Great job!

This Saturday let's meet at 10 A.M. in Big Mountain Park and hunt for signs of Bigfoot together. Bring your friends, your teacher, and your mom!

Dr. Vincent

Chapter 6

Back to the Park

Luke couldn't wait to meet Dr. Vincent at the park that Saturday. He had so many questions to ask about Bigfoot!

Before leaving for the park, Luke made sure he had everything he wanted to show Dr. Vincent. He wondered what the cryptozoologist would say about the hair and the plaster footprint. Those were the only clues they hadn't been able to post on the Web site.

That Saturday morning, Dr. Williams, Mrs.
Delgado, and the kids drove to Big Mountain Park.
As they came through the gates, they saw Mr.
Baxter, the park naturalist.

"Hi, everyone!" Mr. Baxter called to them.
"Good to see you back!"

"We're meeting Dr. Vincent," Luke told him as
he approached the car. "Have you seen him?"

"Oh, Dr. Vincent's been here for hours," Mr.
Baxter told them. "Take a look around. You'll
probably see him. Maybe I'll see you later!"

"Thanks!" called the kids.

Dr. Williams parked the car, and everyone climbed out, eager to meet the cryptozoologist.

Wendy looked around. "Where do you think Dr. Vincent is?" she asked.

Luke had an idea. "It seems most people see Bigfoot near the woods. Maybe we'll find Dr. Vincent there."

"Maybe we'll find Bigfoot there!" Steve joked.

The sun shone brightly overhead as the kids, Mrs. Delgado, and Dr. Williams made their way toward the bushes at the base of the hill where Luke had seen Bigfoot. Suddenly, a tall figure wandered out of the woods. The creature waved its long arms as it moved through the bushes. Everyone stopped and stared.

Dr. Williams held up her hand to keep everyone from talking. "Luke," she said softly, "is that what you saw the other day?"

Luke stared hard at the tall form moving slowly ahead of them. He thought for a minute. "No, it isn't," he said firmly.

"He's right!" called a voice.

When the kids turned around, they saw Mr. Baxter headed toward them. "You've got good eyes, Luke," he said.

"So who—or what—is *that*?" Wendy asked.

Mr. Baxter cupped his hands and shouted to the creature. "Come out here, you joker!"

The tall figure stopped and pulled at the top of his head with one hand. A mask came off the creature's head.

"Dr. Vincent?" Luke asked.

"That's me," said the man, smiling. "Please excuse my strange clothes!" He laughed as he moved closer to show what he was wearing. The suit covered him all over. It was made of a strange brown material with big boots.

"What were you doing?" asked Steve. "Trying to fool us?"

"No, not at all," Dr. Vincent said. "I was just trying to prove your point, Luke." Dr. Vincent turned to Dr. Williams. "Tell them what I'm wearing," he told her.

Dr. Williams nodded. "It's the lab's new extreme weather suit."

"Luke knew it wasn't Bigfoot!" cried Wendy.

"Exactly," said Dr. Vincent. "Luke didn't see someone trying out the suit that day. If he had, he would have thought I was Bigfoot. We needed to make sure of that, and surprising you was the best way to do it."

"Does this prove we saw Bigfoot?" Steve asked.

Dr. Vincent sighed. "If only things were that easy! I believe you saw him, boys, just as I did."

Luke and Steve gave each other high fives.

"From the scientist's point of view, however, we have a lot to prove," he added. "We have the video with its blurry picture of some sort of creature, but what about physical evidence?"

"Show him the hair!" Susan told Luke.

Luke pulled the plastic bag from his pocket. Dr. Vincent put on his glasses, carefully opened the bag, and looked inside.

"Very good," he said as he examined the dark hair. "A lab can check if this is hair or fur from an animal we'd find around here."

"It's not from any animal we can identify," Dr. Williams explained. "We tested it at the lab."

Dr. Vincent turned to the kids. "So what do you think it is?"

Luke thought for a minute. "It may be from an animal we can't identify, an animal we haven't discovered yet."

Dr. Vincent smiled. "That's cryptozoology."

"Hey," Wendy called from the edge of the woods. "Look over here!"

Everyone went over to where Wendy was pointing. "Footprints! Are they Bigfoot's?"

Dr. Vincent leaned over for a look. "They're certainly big enough."

"Wait a minute!" Luke said. He took the plaster cast of the footprint out of his backpack.

He placed it beside the footprint on the ground. "They're not the same, see?" he pointed. "These new prints have four toes, not five."

Dr. Vincent looked up at the kids. "What do you think?" he asked.

"Whatever made these prints is not the creature we saw last week or the one that made the footprints over by the bushes!" replied Steve.

"Then what is it?" asked Dr. Vincent.

"Let's follow the footprints and find out!" cried Wendy, already on her way into the woods.

"Wait!" Mr. Baxter called. "Let's move slowly and stay together! We don't know what we're following yet."

The group walked through the trees, following the footprints. The tracks led to a clearing where the kids saw two young men. They both held long poles with strange shapes attached to the ends.

Luke's eyes got wide. The men were making footprints!

Chapter 7

Fake Footprints

"Hey!" shouted Luke. "What do you think you're doing?"

The two young men stopped and looked at them in surprise.

"Just a minute, Luke," Dr. Vincent said. "I know these fellows. They're students of mine."

Dr. Vincent walked into the clearing. The young men looked at each other and shook their heads. "Uh-oh," one said.

"What's going on?" asked Dr. Vincent.

"We're sorry, Dr. V," said one. "Bob and I just wanted to give you a laugh."

Dr. Vincent frowned. "By fooling me with fake footprints?" he asked.

"We weren't trying to fool you!" Bob said quickly. "It's for . . ." He sighed. "Well, I guess we've got to tell him, Cal."

"It was going to be such a great surprise," Cal groaned. "They'll all be here soon, and we ruined the whole thing."

"Wait a minute," Dr. Vincent said, and held up his hand. "Does this have anything to do with the fact that it's my birthday today?"

"We were going to yell *surprise* when you got here," Bob said. "Instead *you* surprised *us*."

"Why did you make fake footprints?" Karen wanted to know.

"It was because of that school Web site, The River City Almanac," Cal explained.

Karen laughed. "That's our Web site!"

"Everyone's talking about Bigfoot," Cal went on. "Of course, we know Dr. V is really interested in Bigfoot."

"So we thought we'd have a Bigfoot birthday party for him," added Bob. He held up the sticks. "With footprints and everything!" he said.

"It's a great idea, guys. Thanks," Dr. Vincent said, smiling. He looked back at the kids. "I think my friends have a few questions for you."

Luke stepped forward. "I know these footprints are fake, but did you make other footprints about a week ago?"

"No," Cal said. "We got the idea after the Bigfoot posting on the Web site."

"Feel better, Luke?" asked Wendy.

"I guess so," Luke said with a shrug. "How do I know for sure that the footprints I saw were really Bigfoot's?"

"You can't know for sure, Luke," Dr. Vincent replied.

"The park is full of people and animals, Luke," Mr. Baxter said. "They all leave signs of some kind." He pointed to their own footprints and the wheel tracks of Susan's wheelchair. "We know what these tracks are, but you found some tracks we can't explain."

"You also saw something we can't explain," Dr. Williams added.

Luke sighed. "I'm not sure what I saw."

"That's what makes cryptozoology so hard, Luke," said Dr. Vincent. "We have to keep looking and keep trying, don't we?"

"Even if Bigfoot isn't real?" Luke asked.

"Bigfoot is real, Luke!" his sister Susan replied. "It's a real part of our lives."

"It's a real part of River City history, too!" Karen said. "Look how many people posted news about their own sightings on our Web site."

Dr. Vincent nodded. "Your River City Almanac proved that." He turned to Luke. "Nature is full of mysteries. You've found a big one. Think about it. Find out more about it. You may be part of solving the mystery."

"Well," Luke said as he put on his backpack, "I think I may be done here for today, at least."

He turned to go, then looked back. "Happy birthday, Dr. V!" he called. The other kids joined in.

"Thanks, everyone," Dr. Vincent called. "We'll meet again!"

Luke led the way out of the clearing and through the trees. On the way he looked down at the fake footprints. He laughed softly and shook his head.

The kids soon came to the edge of the forest. While the others walked on toward the car, Luke stopped for a minute. He looked back toward the forest. Suddenly he saw a tall figure slip out from between the trees. It raised a long arm toward Luke, as if it were waving to him.

Luke's eyes got wide as he watched. "Hey, wait," he called out to the others, trying to be quiet. They had gone too far down the path to hear him. Luke quickly looked back into the trees. He could still see the figure. "HEY!" he called more loudly, hoping to get someone's attention.

"What?" he heard Steve yelling to him from the parking lot.

Luke started to yell that he could see Bigfoot, but when he turned back to the tree, the creature had vanished. Luke smiled and walked on to the car.

Glossary

contaminating   [kun TAM un ayt ihng] the act of making something impure by bringing it in contact with something that is dirty or harmful

cryptozoologist   [krihp toh zoh AHL uh jist] a scientist who studies animals that are not often seen

evidence   [EV uh duns] something that shows or proves, or that gives a reason for believing

legend   [LEJ und] a story handed down through the years that may or may not be connected to a real event

narrate   [NAR ayt] to give the story of something in writing or speech; to tell what has happened

naturalist   [NACH rul ihst] a person who studies the outside world, especially plants and animals

plaster cast   [PLAS tur kast] an exact copy of something, such as an animal track, made out of a mixture that hardens when dry

posting   [POHST ihng] information that is displayed

traces   [TRAY suz] signs left by someone or something; also, a very small amount of something

Web site   [web syte] a place on the World Wide Web or Internet with one or more computer pages of information